TOMATO PLANT GIRL

A Play for Young Audiences
by
WESLEY MIDDLETON

Dramatic Publishing
Woodstock, Illinois • England • Australia • New Zealand

IMPORTANT BILLING AND CREDIT REQUIREMENTS

All producers of the play *must* give credit to the author(s) of the play in all programs distributed in connection with performances of the play and in all instances in which the title of the play appears for purposes of advertising, publicizing or otherwise exploiting the play and/or a production. The name of the author(s) *must* also appear on a separate line, on which no other name appears, immediately following the title, and *must* appear in size of type not less than fifty percent the size of the title type. Biographical information on the author(s), if included in this book, may be used on all programs. *On all programs this notice must appear:*

"Produced by special arrangement with
THE DRAMATIC PUBLISHING COMPANY of Woodstock, Illinois"

Tomato Plant Girl was originally produced and premiered by Metro Theater Company, St. Louis, Mo., Carol North, Producing Director, and Idaho Theatre for Youth, Boise, Idaho, Pamela Sterling, Artistic Director with major support from the Theatre for Youth Endowment at the University of Texas at Austin.

Metro Theater Company, Fall 1998

Bossy Best Friend . . . . Carlyn Armintrout
Little Girl . . . . Monica Holeczy
Tomato Plant Girl . . . . Kate Frank
The Facilitator . . . . Eddie Webb
(role specific to Metro Theater Company production)

Director: Carol North
Assistant Director/Music Director: Christopher Gurr
Composer: Al Fisher
Costume Designer: Clyde Ruffin
Set Designer: Nicholas Kryah and Jennifer Cassidy
Props: Jennifer Cassidy
Dramaturg: Suzan Zeder
Associate Dramaturg: Tamara Goldbogen

Idaho Theatre for Youth, Spring 1999

Bossy Best Friend . . . . Karen Wennstrom
Little Girl . . . . Leonda Clendenen
Tomato Plant Girl . . . . Sara Bruner

Director: Pamela Sterling
Production Manager: Monica Coburn
Composer/Music Director: Michael Keck
Costume Designer: Anne Hoste
Set Designer: Dean Panttaja
Dramaturg: Tamara Goldbogen

TOMATO PLANT GIRL

A Play for Young Audiences
For 3 Women
(may be expanded with "stagehand" roles)

CHARACTERS

LITTLE GIRL: A small girl, about 10 years old. Recently moved to Heretown from Thereville. Loves books and tomatoes.

BOSSY BEST FRIEND: Older, richer and girlier than Little Girl. Has always lived in Heretown. Loves Barbies and clothes.

TOMATO PLANT GIRL: A tomato spirit who appears in Heretown in the shape of a girl. Does not understand Heretown's rules.

VOICE OF BOSSY BEST FRIEND'S MOTHER

SETTING: Heretown, a small American town where foreigners are suspicious and rules are important.

TIME: Summertime.

Set requirements: Simple tourable set, props.
Approximate running time: 60 minutes

TOMATO PLANT GIRL

SCENE 1

SETTING: *The action takes place in a makeshift garden. The garden is a fenced vacant lot on a small-town residential street. It belongs to LITTLE GIRL and BOSSY BEST FRIEND. Mostly BOSSY BEST FRIEND. There are two tomato plants in the garden. One is dry and wilted. A sign beside it says: "DO NOT TOUCH!" The other is healthy and green, with a single young tomato.*

AT RISE: *We hear the sound of quick, rhythmic ticking. BOSSY BEST FRIEND enters. Everything matches on BOSSY BEST FRIEND: her cute summer dress, the big bow in her hair, her bag. She carries a parasol to shade her from the sun. BOSSY BEST FRIEND looks around the garden. Takes a deep breath. Smiles. Consults her big plastic watch.*

BOSSY BEST FRIEND
Four fifty-eight and thirty seconds.
(She straightens her bow. Looks back at her watch.)
Four fifty-eight and forty-eight seconds.
Four fifty-eight and forty-nine seconds.
(She looks off, then back at her watch.)
Four fifty-eight and fifty-two seconds. Fifty-three. Fifty-four. Fifty—

(LITTLE GIRL runs in, excited and anxious. She wears overall shorts, a T-shirt and a hat. She carries a big book, Tales of Tomatoes, *with a tomato on the cover.)*

LITTLE GIRL

Five? Is it five o'clock?

(BOSSY BEST FRIEND holds out her watch, points at it, then hides it, fast. She's lying.)

BOSSY BEST FRIEND

And 10 seconds.
You're late!

LITTLE GIRL

I was reading!

BOSSY BEST FRIEND

You're *late*.

LITTLE GIRL

About tomatoes! *(Holding out the book.)* Grandma gave it to me. When she was alive.

BOSSY BEST FRIEND

Poor dear. Put it out of your mind.

(BOSSY BEST FRIEND tries to take the book. LITTLE GIRL holds on.)

LITTLE GIRL

We could read to the plants!

BOSSY BEST FRIEND

It is *not* time to read!
Give me the book *now*, Booknose. *Please.*

(LITTLE GIRL lets BOSSY BEST FRIEND take the book.
BOSSY BEST FRIEND puts it with her things.)

LITTLE GIRL

Grandma used to read to me.

BOSSY BEST FRIEND

Well, maybe you'll meet *my* grandma someday.

LITTLE GIRL

Really?

BOSSY BEST FRIEND

If you're a *very* good friend. We'll see.
Now hurry. We're late for your favorite game!
(BOSSY BEST FRIEND smiles and claps twice.)
Mother May I!
(LITTLE GIRL, who does like this game, walks several
paces away from BOSSY BEST FRIEND and turns to
face her.)
Ready?
Good. Two queenly curtsies.

LITTLE GIRL

Mother may I?

BOSSY BEST FRIEND

Yes you may.

(LITTLE GIRL curtsies twice.)
Lovely!
Three ballerina twirls.

LITTLE GIRL

Mother may I?

BOSSY BEST FRIEND

Yes you may.
(LITTLE GIRL does three twirls.)
Gorgeous!
Five giant steps.

LITTLE GIRL

Mother may I?

BOSSY BEST FRIEND

Yes you may.
(LITTLE GIRL starts giant-stepping toward BOSSY BEST FRIEND.)
Backward.
(LITTLE GIRL freezes mid-step, then steps backward with the same foot, almost losing her balance. She does the five steps.)
Now hop eight times on your lefthand foot.
Forward. Hurry up!

LITTLE GIRL

Mother may I?

BOSSY BEST FRIEND

Yes you may.

(LITTLE GIRL starts to hop. BOSSY BEST FRIEND interrupts.)

Now stand on your tippy tiptoes and eat dirt!

(LITTLE GIRL quickly picks up some dirt, stands on tiptoe, and starts to bring the dirt to her lips.)

Ha! Quit, silly girl! We don't eat dirt!

LITTLE GIRL *(freezes)*

I forgot.

BOSSY BEST FRIEND

Poor Booknose. Still—you did *very* well.

You get a gold star!

(BOSSY BEST FRIEND takes a big gold star from her pocket and sticks it on LITTLE GIRL's forehead.)

Ta-da!

(They do a very proper "buddy" handshake.)

BOSSY BEST FRIEND, LITTLE GIRL

Best friends forever—Number One!

(LITTLE GIRL smiles proudly and curtsies, removing her hat. As she does, she feels the sun on her face and hair.)

LITTLE GIRL

Mmmm.

(She closes her eyes, stretches upward, breathes.)

The sun!

BOSSY BEST FRIEND

Booknose! *Careful!* The ultraviolent rays!

                        LITTLE GIRL
But—

                        BOSSY BEST FRIEND
Sunburn is *wrong!* Put on your hat!
        (LITTLE GIRL puts on her hat.)
Now. What time is it?

                        LITTLE GIRL
Book time!

                        BOSSY BEST FRIEND
No—

                        LITTLE GIRL
Tomato plant time!

                        BOSSY BEST FRIEND
No. Not five-fifteen.
What time is it?

                        LITTLE GIRL
Barbie.

*(BOSSY BEST FRIEND smiles, snaps her fingers once.
LITTLE GIRL gets in place for the game. BOSSY BEST
FRIEND takes out two Barbies. One wears a fancy
dress. The other wears a plain dress and has bad hair.
BOSSY BEST FRIEND hands the latter Barbie to LIT-
TLE GIRL.)*

BOSSY BEST FRIEND

You're this one.

LITTLE GIRL

I know.

(BOSSY BEST FRIEND and LITTLE GIRL place their Barbies in stiff standing positions.)

BOSSY BEST FRIEND

One-two-three!

(Both speak, in quick rhythm, as their Barbies.)

BOSSY BEST FRIEND

Dena!

LITTLE GIRL

Lena!

(The Barbies cheek-kiss loudly, three times. Rhythm: "Dena! Lena! Kiss kiss kiss!")

LITTLE GIRL

How are you?

BOSSY BEST FRIEND

Just grand!

LITTLE GIRL

And your job?

BOSSY BEST FRIEND

Unsurpassed!

LITTLE GIRL

And your boyfriends?

BOSSY BEST FRIEND

Ooh la!

LITTLE GIRL

You look lovely.

BOSSY BEST FRIEND

Can't hear you!

LITTLE GIRL

Just *lovely*.

BOSSY BEST FRIEND

Why thanks.
Are you wearing that dress to my party tonight?

LITTLE GIRL

Of course.

BOSSY BEST FRIEND

But it's ugly!

LITTLE GIRL

Oh. Then I'll wear—a satin ball gown with rose petticoats!

BOSSY BEST FRIEND

You can't have a new dress!

LITTLE GIRL *(as herself)*

But I've got a gold star!

BOSSY BEST FRIEND *(as her Barbie)*

Guess all the young beaus will be looking at me!

LITTLE GIRL

Beaus?

BOSSY BEST FRIEND

Young *beaus*. At the party! The *boys!*

LITTLE GIRL

Oh.

BOSSY BEST FRIEND

You're jealous!

LITTLE GIRL *(matter of fact)*

I'm not.

BOSSY BEST FRIEND

Yes you are.

LITTLE GIRL *(as before)*

No. You can go. I'll read.

(LITTLE GIRL reaches for her book. BOSSY BEST FRIEND stops her, snatches her Barbie.)

> BOSSY BEST FRIEND *(as herself)*

Your Barbie loves parties and would *die* for a beau. Your
Barbie wants what *my* Barbie wants but *my* Barbie can
have it and your Barbie can't. That's the game! Now what
do you say?

> LITTLE GIRL

I'm sorry.

> BOSSY BEST FRIEND

What time is it?

> LITTLE GIRL

Tomato plant—

> BOSSY BEST FRIEND

NO!!
  (BOSSY BEST FRIEND composes herself to lecture.)
Booknose: who were you three months ago?

  (LITTLE GIRL starts to speak.)

> BOSSY BEST FRIEND

You were no one. You were the new girl, just moved here
from Thereville. Always alone—reading, walking, talking
to plants...till I found you and told you: you need a friend.
I taught you not to act like a *(lowers her voice) foreigner.*

  *(LITTLE GIRL gasps at the word. BOSSY BEST FRIEND
  points to LITTLE GIRL; LITTLE GIRL recites the defini-
  tion with military precision.)*

LITTLE GIRL

Foreigner: Anyone who looks acts speaks appears seems or suggests themselves to be in any way different from the glorious ways of the virtuous people of Heretown!

BOSSY BEST FRIEND

You're lucky I've taught you. Don't forget to play right. You're this one.

(She holds out LITTLE GIRL's Barbie. LITTLE GIRL looks at her, doesn't take it.)

What?

LITTLE GIRL *(matter of fact)*

It's tomato plant time.

BOSSY BEST FRIEND

You're *this* one!

LITTLE GIRL

It's time! It's past five-fifteen!

(Reluctantly, BOSSY BEST FRIEND checks her watch.)

BOSSY BEST FRIEND *(annoyed)*

All right. No Barbie.

(BOSSY BEST FRIEND puts the Barbies in the bag.)

You'll do better next time. Now—

LITTLE GIRL

Now for the glorious harvest! Hurrah!

(LITTLE GIRL starts to run toward her planter.)

BOSSY BEST FRIEND

Hold your little ponies.
(LITTLE GIRL stops.)
We go at the *same* time. Remember?

(Slowly, the two turn together toward the garden plots and walk toward them. They stand in front of their respective garden plots. Both gasp.)

BOSSY BEST FRIEND.

Oh! This can't be right!

LITTLE GIRL

Wow. Velvet green leaves and flowers of gold!
Look! Come look.

BOSSY BEST FRIEND *(approaches the plant)*

Well, Little Girl. What a *beautiful* plant.
Look at mine.

LITTLE GIRL

Oh! It's—um, it's—

BOSSY BEST FRIEND

Dead. It's *dead*.
It's all your fault.

LITTLE GIRL

My fault?

BOSSY BEST FRIEND *(mocking her)*

"Put it in the sun!"

LITTLE GIRL
Sun's good for them!

BOSSY BEST FRIEND
It's withered!

LITTLE GIRL
Did you water it?

BOSSY BEST FRIEND
What?

LITTLE GIRL
Plants need water!

BOSSY BEST FRIEND
Since when?

LITTLE GIRL
I told you!

BOSSY BEST FRIEND
You don't water yours.

LITTLE GIRL
I do.

(BOSSY BEST FRIEND is shocked. LITTLE GIRL realizes she said the wrong thing.)

BOSSY BEST FRIEND
You've been coming in *secret* to water your plant?

LITTLE GIRL
To make sure it lived.

BOSSY BEST FRIEND
And make sure mine died!

LITTLE GIRL
No!

BOSSY BEST FRIEND
You didn't water *my* plant.

LITTLE GIRL
You said never touch it! You said "DO NOT TOUCH!"

BOSSY BEST FRIEND
Give me your plant.

LITTLE GIRL *(shocked)*
I couldn't!

BOSSY BEST FRIEND
If I had a gorgeous green plant, Little Girl, and yours was wilted and withered and dead, I'd give you my plant if you wanted it.
   (LITTLE GIRL says nothing.)
Little Girl?

LITTLE GIRL
I wouldn't want that.

BOSSY BEST FRIEND

But I would do it—because I'm your *friend*.
Just like you're mine.
You *are* my friend. Aren't you?

LITTLE GIRL

Yes. I'm your friend.

BOSSY BEST FRIEND

So give me your plant!
   (LITTLE GIRL wrings her hands.)
Little Girl—*please?*

LITTLE GIRL

The plant is precious.

BOSSY BEST FRIEND

The plant will be fine.

LITTLE GIRL

Will you water it?

BOSSY BEST FRIEND

Little Girl: I'm your friend!
What's more important? Me or the plant?

   *(LITTLE GIRL looks at the plant. BOSSY BEST FRIEND
   glares at her. LITTLE GIRL gives in.)*

LITTLE GIRL

When we move it, we have to be careful. OK?

BOSSY BEST FRIEND

Good, Little Girl! You did the right thing.

    (BOSSY BEST FRIEND pats LITTLE GIRL on the shoulder. Then smiles at the plant.)

Now, tomato plant: this won't hurt a bit. We'll just move you to my pretty side of the garden. We'll do that right now. Together.

    (BOSSY BEST FRIEND looks at LITTLE GIRL. LITTLE GIRL helps, reluctantly. BOSSY BEST FRIEND points to LITTLE GIRL's plant. LITTLE GIRL carefully uproots it. BOSSY BEST FRIEND plucks up the dead plant from her own planter and pitches it over her shoulder, out of the garden—preferably offstage. [It must be offstage by the start of Scene 2.] Then she takes LITTLE GIRL's plant from her, and crudely replants it in her own planter.)

LITTLE GIRL

Careful!

BOSSY BEST FRIEND

All done!

    (LITTLE GIRL hovers, worried, over the plant. BOSSY BEST FRIEND stands in front of it, moving her out of the way. She smiles at LITTLE GIRL.)

Thank you for your beautiful gift.

LITTLE GIRL

Gift?

BOSSY BEST FRIEND

Of course. You gave it to me.

LITTLE GIRL *(confused)*

But you made me—

BOSSY BEST FRIEND
(gives LITTLE GIRL her book)

Okay, Booknose. That's all for today. *(Sweetly.)* Here's your
book. Time to go read!
*(LITTLE GIRL takes the book, looks back at the plant.
BOSSY BEST FRIEND moves her off.)*

Toodle-oo! See you tomorrow! Bye-bye!
*(LITTLE GIRL goes, looking back at the plant. BOSSY
BEST FRIEND preens and admires the plant.)*

Mm-hm. Mm-hm. Mm-hm. Ooh, lovely plant! Now you're
all *mine!*
(BOSSY BEST FRIEND blows her plant a kiss, then exits.)

SCENE 2

*(The next day. LITTLE GIRL runs onstage with a water-
ing can. She checks to make sure BOSSY BEST FRIEND
isn't there, then rushes to the plant.)*

LITTLE GIRL

Oh, poor plant!
You're thirsty!

*(LITTLE GIRL raises the watering can, about to water
the plant. The sound of quick, rhythmic ticking. LITTLE
GIRL freezes. BOSSY BEST FRIEND enters, carrying
her bag.)*

BOSSY BEST FRIEND

You're early!

It's four fifty-nine.

   (*BOSSY BEST FRIEND puts her hand out for the watering can, clears her throat. LITTLE GIRL hands it over.*)

Thank you.

LITTLE GIRL

The plant—

BOSSY BEST FRIEND

The plant is fine.

LITTLE GIRL

It's unhappy!

BOSSY BEST FRIEND

I watered it.

LITTLE GIRL

When?

BOSSY BEST FRIEND

Last night.

LITTLE GIRL

Are you sure?

BOSSY BEST FRIEND (*points at her watch*)

Oh my. Look at the time!

Come on, Little Girl: your favorite game!

(BOSSY BEST FRIEND claps twice. LITTLE GIRL steps into position for the start of Mother May I. She does not stop looking at the plant.)

BOSSY BEST FRIEND

Ready? Good.
Five helicopter twirls.

LITTLE GIRL

Mother may I?

BOSSY BEST FRIEND

Yes you may.
   (LITTLE GIRL starts doing big twirls toward the plant.)
This way! Stop! Start over!
   (LITTLE GIRL stops. BOSSY BEST FRIEND glares, then claps twice.)
Now. Three teeny-tiny baby steps.

LITTLE GIRL

Mother may I?

BOSSY BEST FRIEND

Yes you may.
   (LITTLE GIRL does the steps, bigger than usual, moving toward the plant.)
Booknose!
   (BOSSY BEST FRIEND stands between LITTLE GIRL and the plant.)
No more game. Barbie time.

(BOSSY BEST FRIEND snaps her fingers once. She takes the Barbies from the bag and holds out the one with bad hair.)
You're this one.

LITTLE GIRL

I know.

BOSSY BEST FRIEND

One—two—three!

(As Barbies.)

BOSSY BEST FRIEND

Dena!

LITTLE GIRL

Lena!

(Kiss-kiss-kiss.)

LITTLE GIRL

How are you?

BOSSY BEST FRIEND *(as an adjective)*

Ladeda!

LITTLE GIRL

And your job?

BOSSY BEST FRIEND

Tip-top.

LITTLE GIRL

And your plant?

BOSSY BEST FRIEND

My *what?*

LITTLE GIRL

Your tomato plant!

(BOSSY BEST FRIEND grabs LITTLE GIRL's Barbie.)

BOSSY BEST FRIEND *(as herself)*

NO! That's not it! That is not how we play!
Dumb tomato plant girl. Dumb like a plant!
*(Tears start down LITTLE GIRL's cheeks. She turns
away to hide them.)*
Are you crying?

LITTLE GIRL

No.

BOSSY BEST FRIEND
(wipes a tear off LITTLE GIRL's cheek)
Yes you are. Only foreigners cry!
(She hands LITTLE GIRL a hanky.)
Here. Hurry up. Don't let anyone see!
*(LITTLE GIRL dries her tears. BOSSY BEST FRIEND
grabs the hanky back.)*
And don't be a worry wart. My plant will be fine.
Of course, it will miss me when I go away—

LITTLE GIRL

You're going away?

BOSSY BEST FRIEND

To my grandma's.

LITTLE GIRL *(wistful)*

Oh.

BOSSY BEST FRIEND *(gloating)*

Back-to-school shopping! It could take a week.

LITTLE GIRL

But the plant—

BOSSY BEST FRIEND

Will miss me. But it will be *fine*.

LITTLE GIRL

I'll take care of it.

BOSSY BEST FRIEND

No.

LITTLE GIRL

But you can't—

BOSSY BEST FRIEND

Little Girl: I can do what I like! I can water the plant or
leave it be. I can pick the fruit, I can preen the vine, I can
perfume the flowers—I can pluck off a leaf!

*(BOSSY BEST FRIEND plucks off a leaf, crumples it,
and tosses it into the air.)*
It's my plant! It lives for me!
*(LITTLE GIRL gasps, in shock, and covers her mouth
with her hands.)*
What climbed up *your* nostril?
(LITTLE GIRL, mouth still covered, makes a noise of distress.)
Little *Girl—*

*(Sound of quick, rhythmic ticking. BOSSY BEST FRIEND's
MOTHER calls from offstage. BOSSY BEST FRIEND
jumps and freezes.)*

BOSSY BEST FRIEND'S MOTHER
(recorded; snooty, agitated)
*Dar—*ling!

LITTLE GIRL
Your mother.

BOSSY BEST FRIEND
Shut up!
(To MOTHER, nervous.) Yes ma'am!

BOSSY BEST FRIEND'S MOTHER *(off)*
Grandma's waiting!

BOSSY BEST FRIEND *(gathers her things)*
Yes ma'am!
(To LITTLE GIRL.) I'll be back.

BOSSY BEST FRIEND'S MOTHER *(off)*
Darling!

BOSSY BEST FRIEND
(To MOTHER.) Yes ma'am!
(To LITTLE GIRL.) And don't you forget—

BOSSY BEST FRIEND'S MOTHER *(off)*
You're *late!*

BOSSY BEST FRIEND
If you *touch* my new plant—

BOSSY BEST FRIEND'S MOTHER *(off)*
If you're late for Grandma—

BOSSY BEST FRIEND
I'll rip up your book and feed it to my poodle!

BOSSY BEST FRIEND'S MOTHER *(off)*
I'll melt down those Barbies and serve them for dinner.

BOSSY BEST FRIEND & MOTHER
We wouldn't want *that* to happen.

BOSSY BEST FRIEND *(to MOTHER)*
I'm coming!

BOSSY BEST FRIEND'S MOTHER *(off)*
Hurry up!

BOSSY BEST FRIEND *(to LITTLE GIRL)*
Be good!

BOSSY BEST FRIEND & MOTHER
Now do as I say, dearie. Or else!

(BOSSY BEST FRIEND runs off. LITTLE GIRL watches her go, then explodes.)

LITTLE GIRL
Oooh wicked badness meanmeanmean tomato-hating leaf-killing evil rudeness jerk!
(LITTLE GIRL claps her hand over her mouth. She can't believe what she just said. Then she kneels near the tomato plant.)
Oh plant—I won't let you suffer. I'll replant you on my good side of the garden.
(LITTLE GIRL closes her eyes.)
Okay.
(LITTLE GIRL puts her hands around the stem.)
(To the plant.) Ready?
(To herself.) Ready.
One—
two—
three.
(LITTLE GIRL begins to pull up the plant. But the root system has grown. It is yards and yards long. Endless.)
All these *roots!*
(LITTLE GIRL keeps pulling up roots. A low, vibrating sound—the Earthsoil Hum—fills the garden. LITTLE GIRL looks around, a bit scared.)
What's that noise?

(The roots start coming more slowly. Something heavy is attached to the roots, moving upward with them, through the soil.)

What's *that*?

(LITTLE GIRL pulls harder. The ends of the roots emerge, clutched in two small hands. Arms and shoulders follow—)

Ohh—

(Then a face: the face of TOMATO PLANT GIRL. She is messy, dirt-covered. Her eyes are closed. She is totally new to her body.)

WHOA!

(Stunned, LITTLE GIRL lets go of the roots, reeling backward. TOMATO PLANT GIRL opens her eyes, lets go of the roots, and opens her mouth; she spits out dirt and a burst of sound. [The words should not sound like words.])

TOMATO PLANT GIRL

Ooohtomatomeanmeanmeansufferleafplantreadyonetworoot!

(TOMATO PLANT GIRL and LITTLE GIRL are both startled by the sound. LITTLE GIRL gasps. TOMATO PLANT GIRL slowly moves her head till she sees LITTLE GIRL. TOMATO PLANT GIRL looks at her and bursts into laughter. After some hesitation, LITTLE GIRL, still nervous, starts laughing too. TOMATO PLANT GIRL laughs so hard that she cries. Then she actually starts to cry. She looks at the strange world around her and big red tears roll down her cheeks.)

LITTLE GIRL

Don't cry. Only foreigners cry!

Stop! Stop! Don't let anyone see!

(TOMATO PLANT GIRL doesn't stop. Anxious, LITTLE GIRL hesitates, then gathers resolve. LITTLE GIRL wipes a tear from TOMATO PLANT GIRL's cheek. She steps back and looks at the tear.)

Red!

(LITTLE GIRL looks at TOMATO PLANT GIRL. Very cautiously, she tastes the tear.)

(With wonder.) Tomato.

(TOMATO PLANT GIRL picks up a handful of dirt, then hums and lets it fall through her fingers. She is calling the Earthsoil Hum. The Earthsoil Hum returns. TOMATO PLANT GIRL welcomes the hum with a gesture, closes her eyes and hums with it.)

LITTLE GIRL

What is it? What's that sound?

(TOMATO PLANT GIRL keeps humming, eyes closed. LIT-TLE GIRL covers her ears, steps away from TOMATO PLANT GIRL.)

I'm sure you're very nice and from a very nice place, and I'd like to welcome you and show you around, but I can't.

(TOMATO PLANT GIRL keeps humming, eyes closed.)

So—I'm sure you have to go, and when I get back, you'll be gone. And I'll replant the plant, and everything will be fine.

(The Earthsoil Hum fades. TOMATO PLANT GIRL opens her eyes. Looks at LITTLE GIRL.)

LITTLE GIRL

I have to go now. It's dinner time. Mom-Dad-table-TV!
Nice to meet you. Have a good trip! Goodbye!

*(LITTLE GIRL rushes off. TOMATO PLANT GIRL
emerges fully from the earth. She moves and makes sounds
as she discovers her new body. She tastes some of the
garden dirt: it's too dry. As she spits it out, she discovers her tongue. She realizes she is thirsty. TOMATO
PLANT GIRL looks at the sky. Then, with purposeful gestures, she calls on the rain [It does not come.] TOMATO
PLANT GIRL continues this movement until LITTLE GIRL
approaches.)*

SCENE 3

*(The same night. About an hour later. The uprooted to-
mato plant from Scene 2 and its long roots are in a pile
on the ground. LITTLE GIRL approaches the garden. She
carries a watering can and flowerpot. She's nervous.)*

LITTLE GIRL *(continuous, as she enters)*

Is she here is she here is she here is she here is she here is
she here?

*(At the sound of the voice, TOMATO PLANT GIRL hides.
LITTLE GIRL looks, quickly, for TOMATO PLANT GIRL.
Doesn't see her.)*

Ha! She's not here!

(LITTLE GIRL approaches the dead plant.)

She's not here and now I can help my poor plant! Look, plant—look what I've got! It's Mom's best topsoil! With minerals! Yum!

(LITTLE GIRL attempts to replant the dead plant. She reaches into the flowerpot for topsoil, sprinkling it on the roots. TOMATO PLANT GIRL emerges from hiding and begins to eat topsoil from the pot, unseen by LITTLE GIRL.)

See? It'll put you in tip-top shape. My best friend will come back, and she'll be so happy—

(LITTLE GIRL reaches back into the flowerpot and accidentally touches TOMATO PLANT GIRL's hand. She shrieks. She doesn't look at TOMATO PLANT GIRL.)

Go away. You're not here!

(TOMATO PLANT GIRL eats another handful of dirt, looks intently at LITTLE GIRL. Slowly, LITTLE GIRL turns to look at TOMATO PLANT GIRL.)

Hey! Hey! *No!* We don't eat *dirt!*

TOMATO PLANT GIRL

Dirrrrrtt.

(TOMATO PLANT GIRL eats noisily and happily. LITTLE GIRL grabs the flowerpot.)

LITTLE GIRL

Don't do that! Dumb tomato plant girl!

(LITTLE GIRL stops, hearing herself.)

(To herself.) Tomato Plant Girl.

(TOMATO PLANT GIRL looks at LITTLE GIRL, confused. LITTLE GIRL picks up the flowerpot, starts to pace.)

I need to line things up in my brain.

(TOMATO PLANT GIRL follows her, tugs on the flower-pot.)

TOMATO PLANT GIRL
Mm.

LITTLE GIRL
What?

TOMATO PLANT GIRL
Mmm. Dirrt.

LITTLE GIRL *(showing her it's empty)*
No. No more. You ate it!
  (TOMATO PLANT GIRL moans.)
Sorry.

TOMATO PLANT GIRL
"Sorry."

LITTLE GIRL *(pointing to herself)*
"I'm sorry."

(TOMATO PLANT GIRL points at LITTLE GIRL, as if "Sorry" is her name.)

TOMATO PLANT GIRL
Sorry.

LITTLE GIRL
No. Sorry. It means—I should have done something, but I didn't. Or I shouldn't have, but I did.

(TOMATO PLANT GIRL looks puzzled.)
It's important.
(Pointing to herself again.) "I'm sorry." It's *important. Big!*

*(LITTLE GIRL does a "big" movement. TOMATO PLANT
GIRL mirrors it, laughs.)*

TOMATO PLANT GIRL

BIG!
*(TOMATO PLANT GIRL points at LITTLE GIRL, makes
the "big" movement.)*
BIG SORR-RRY!

LITTLE GIRL

Shhh!

TOMATO PLANT GIRL

"SHHH!"

LITTLE GIRL

Shhh.

*(In "SHHH!" TOMATO PLANT GIRL hears the sound
of water. She begins to do her rain-calling movement,
now directed at LITTLE GIRL.)*

TOMATO PLANT GIRL

Shhhhhh.

LITTLE GIRL

What? What—you want a shower? Not at my house—*my* shower's clean! My parents work hard and our house is neat. You eat dirt and you dress upside-down!

(TOMATO PLANT GIRL continues the motion, but opens her mouth and tilts her face to the sky.)

What? What?

Oh! *(Pointing to her mouth.)* Drink!

TOMATO PLANT GIRL

Drrrink!

LITTLE GIRL

Drink.

(LITTLE GIRL holds up the watering can and pours water into TOMATO PLANT GIRL's mouth.)

You were thirsty.

(LITTLE GIRL suddenly remembers the [dead] plant.)

Oh! Thirsty!

(LITTLE GIRL rushes to the plant, pours water on it.)

Here, poor plant—

(TOMATO PLANT GIRL follows, tugs on the watering can, points to herself.)

TOMATO PLANT GIRL

Drink.

LITTLE GIRL

No! It's for the plant!

(LITTLE GIRL pours the rest of the water on the plant. TOMATO PLANT GIRL moans and shakes her head, confused.)

Lots of things went backwards and I need to fix them up.
   (LITTLE GIRL kneels next to the plant.)
I need to replant these roots—all these roots—

   *(LITTLE GIRL pushes the rest of the roots underground,
   covering them with soil. TOMATO PLANT GIRL grabs a
   root and looks at LITTLE GIRL.)*

TOMATO PLANT GIRL

Root.

LITTLE GIRL *(puts the root back)*

Root. There. In place.
Ready, plant? One, two, three!
   *(LITTLE GIRL tries to stand the plant up. The plant flops
   over. LITTLE GIRL tries again.)*
(To the plant.) Plant! PLANT! Come on.
You're *not dead.*
You're not dead.

   *(TOMATO PLANT GIRL points to the plant. She is mat-
   ter-of-fact.)*

TOMATO PLANT GIRL

Dead.

LITTLE GIRL *(knowing it's true)*

Not dead.

TOMATO PLANT GIRL *(as before)*

Dead.

(TOMATO PLANT GIRL holds a handful of dirt out to LITTLE GIRL. LITTLE GIRL looks at TOMATO PLANT GIRL. Then at the plant.)

LITTLE GIRL *(slowly accepting it)*

Dead.

(LITTLE GIRL takes the dirt. She helps TOMATO PLANT GIRL bury the plant. They are silent for a moment. The Earthsoil Hum returns. TOMATO PLANT GIRL hears it. As before, she gestures to acknowledge its presence, then hums with it. LITTLE GIRL covers her ears.)

LITTLE GIRL

That hum—

TOMATO PLANT GIRL

Humm.

(LITTLE GIRL cautiously uncovers her ears for a moment, then covers them.)

LITTLE GIRL

It's from down in the earth!

TOMATO PLANT GIRL

Errth.

LITTLE GIRL

Earth ... hum.
(The Earthsoil Hum fades. LITTLE GIRL slowly uncovers her ears. She looks at the buried plant.)

My grandma said, when plants die, they go back to the earth and feed other plants. So they might go away, but they're not really gone.

(LITTLE GIRL looks at TOMATO PLANT GIRL. TOMATO PLANT GIRL looks at LITTLE GIRL.)

TOMATO PLANT GIRL *(agreeing)*
Errth.
(LITTLE GIRL smiles. Then TOMATO PLANT GIRL motions to the watering can and flowerpot.)
Dirrrt ... drrink.

LITTLE GIRL
You eat a lot!

TOMATO PLANT GIRL *(a hungry noise)*
Mmm.

LITTLE GIRL
You need to learn some things.

(TOMATO PLANT GIRL holds the flowerpot and watering can out to LITTLE GIRL.

TOMATO PLANT GIRL
Dirt drink.

LITTLE GIRL
If you're going to stay here—

TOMATO PLANT GIRL

DIRT! DRINK!

LITTLE GIRL

Okay!
(LITTLE GIRL takes the flowerpot and watering can.)
But you have to learn how to play.

TOMATO PLANT GIRL *(confused)*

Mmm?

LITTLE GIRL

Mother May I. I'll teach you tomorrow. Here. At tomato
plant time! Five-fifteen.
(LITTLE GIRL goes.)

TOMATO PLANT GIRL
(calling LITTLE GIRL's "name")

Sorry?
Sorr-rry! Dirt...drink.
*(TOMATO PLANT GIRL turns back to the garden. She
stands and does her rain-calling gesture.)*

SCENE 4

*(The next day. TOMATO PLANT GIRL sits, holding her
belly. She moans. LITTLE GIRL enters with the flowerpot and watering can.)*

LITTLE GIRL

Tomato Plant Girl?

It's time for a game!

(TOMATO PLANT GIRL rushes to the flowerpot and watering can.)

Hey!

Wait.

(LITTLE GIRL holds the flowerpot and watering can in the air so TOMATO PLANT GIRL cannot reach them.)

First you learn to play. Then: dirt and drink.

Okay.

Mother may I!

(LITTLE GIRL claps twice.)

Ready? Good.

Three queenly curtsies!

Watch.

(LITTLE GIRL begins to demonstrate.)

One—two—

(TOMATO PLANT GIRL rushes to the flowerpot, grabs it, eats a handful of dirt.)

No no wait!

You have to play right!

(LITTLE GIRL grabs the flowerpot back. TOMATO PLANT GIRL makes a frustrated noise.)

You didn't say "Mother may I!"

Start over.

Say "Mother may I!"

TOMATO PLANT GIRL

Mmm—mthrrrr—

(TOMATO PLANT GIRL spits out the word, laughs at the sound. LITTLE GIRL creates a hand gesture to represent the words.)

LITTLE GIRL

Here. "*Mother may I!*"
(*LITTLE GIRL does the gesture. TOMATO PLANT GIRL
repeats it.*)
Good!
Now—
(*TOMATO PLANT GIRL, repeating the "Mother may I"
gesture, moves toward the dirt and drink, with no curtsies.*)

TOMATO PLANT GIRL

Mthrr mthrr mthrr—

LITTLE GIRL

No! Curtsy curtsy curtsy!

(*TOMATO PLANT GIRL stops and does one slow curtsy
to LITTLE GIRL.*)

TOMATO PLANT GIRL

Crrrtze.

LITTLE GIRL (*giving in*)

You'll do better next time.

(*LITTLE GIRL gives TOMATO PLANT GIRL a handful
of dirt. TOMATO PLANT GIRL eats avidly. LITTLE GIRL
pours water into TOMATO PLANT GIRL's mouth. TO-
MATO PLANT GIRL, after drinking her fill, holds onto a
big mouthful of water, so she can share a trick with LIT-
TLE GIRL.*)

LITTLE GIRL

Next is ballerina twirl. It's difficult.
(LITTLE GIRL gets into position for the twirl.)
You start like this. Watch carefully.
(Gleefully, TOMATO PLANT GIRL spits a spray of water in the air. It sprinkles down on her and on LITTLE GIRL.)
Hey!

TOMATO PLANT GIRL

Mmmm. Currt-ze!
(TOMATO PLANT GIRL does her own big curtsy of joy.)

LITTLE GIRL

That's not the *game!*

(On "game," LITTLE GIRL makes an emphatic gesture. TOMATO PLANT GIRL repeats the gesture.)

TOMATO PLANT GIRL *(liking the sound)*

Gaaame.

LITTLE GIRL

"Game." It has rules. It's very specific.

(TOMATO PLANT GIRL begins to repeat the "game" gesture, transforming it each time, creating her own game, inviting LITTLE GIRL to join her.)

TOMATO PLANT GIRL *(continuous)*

Gamegamegame—

LITTLE GIRL

One person tells the other: do something. The other asks
  permission: "Mother may I." Then—
What are you doing?

TOMATO PLANT GIRL
(shows LITTLE GIRL the gesture)

Gaaaame.

*(Warily, LITTLE GIRL watches TOMATO PLANT GIRL
and mirrors her gesture. Note: While it should appear to
be improvised, the following action is "very specific." It
is important that the audience see LITTLE GIRL and
TOMATO PLANT GIRL mirroring each other, paying
attention to each other's movements, and transforming
gestures together.)*

TOMATO PLANT GIRL, LITTLE GIRL

Gaaame.

LITTLE GIRL

Right. A game has rules.

*(TOMATO PLANT GIRL moves into a new gesture, an
exaggeration of LITTLE GIRL's gesture from the line,
"A game has rules.")*

TOMATO PLANT GIRL

Gaame ... ruulz!

(LITTLE GIRL is surprised to see herself in TOMATO PLANT GIRL's gesture. She laughs, then transforms the gesture into a new one.)

LITTLE GIRL

Gameruulz!

(Facing each other, they do LITTLE GIRL's gesture together.)

LITTLE GIRL, TOMATO PLANT GIRL

Gameruulz!
(They transform LITTLE GIRL's gesture to create a new gesture together.)
Gaameruulz!

LITTLE GIRL

We made a new game!

(TOMATO PLANT GIRL motions for LITTLE GIRL to stay put. Then she picks up the flowerpot and watering can and moves to where LITTLE GIRL stood during the Mother May I game. TOMATO PLANT GIRL begins to reward LITTLE GIRL. She holds out a handful of dirt.)

TOMATO PLANT GIRL

Dirrrt!
(LITTLE GIRL politely refuses. TOMATO PLANT GIRL eats the dirt, then holds up the watering can.)
Drrink.

(Cautiously, LITTLE GIRL opens her mouth. TOMATO PLANT GIRL pours water in LITTLE GIRL's mouth. LIT-TLE GIRL gets a mouthful of water. She looks impishly at TOMATO PLANT GIRL. She spits the water up in the air—just for a second. LITTLE GIRL takes the watering can and starts to give TOMATO PLANT GIRL a drink. TOMATO PLANT GIRL leads LITTLE GIRL to LITTLE GIRL's side of the garden, where her plant once grew, and stands with her arms outstretched. LITTLE GIRL "wa-ters" TOMATO PLANT GIRL. TOMATO PLANT GIRL starts to grow. The Earthsoil Hum returns. Again, TO-MATO PLANT GIRL acknowledges it with a gesture.)

LITTLE GIRL

The Earth hum!

(As before, LITTLE GIRL covers her ears. TOMATO PLANT GIRL, still turning, begins to grow bigger, red-der, greener.)

Tomato Plant Girl—you're growing!

(LITTLE GIRL removes her hands from her ears and watches the process, amazed.)

Wow!

(TOMATO PLANT GIRL makes one full turn, then yawns and settles to the ground, asleep. LITTLE GIRL sits watching her, intrigued. The sound of quick, rhyth-mic ticking. LITTLE GIRL looks around, nervous. A pink plastic postcard drops from the sky. LITTLE GIRL jumps, then catches the postcard and silently reads.)

VOICE OF BOSSY BEST FRIEND *(off)*

Dear Booknose—Hope you're not too lonely. Don't worry, dear; I miss you too. I'll be back in two days, three hours, and forty-five minutes. In the meantime, be good and keep your hands off my plant!

(LITTLE GIRL looks at TOMATO PLANT GIRL, and at BOSSY BEST FRIEND's side of the garden.)

LITTLE GIRL *(panicked)*

"Keep your hands off my plant—"

Oh no!

(LITTLE GIRL paces, remembering.)

I should have, but I didn't...I shouldn't have, but I did...

"Do as I say—or else!"

Oh no!

(LITTLE GIRL takes a deep breath. Thinks for a moment. Looks at TOMATO PLANT GIRL. Makes a decision. Then picks up the postcard, flowerpot, and watering can. She turns back to the sleeping TOMATO PLANT GIRL.)

Don't go away! I'll be back! I'll be back.

(LITTLE GIRL exits, quickly.)

SCENE 5

(The next day. TOMATO PLANT GIRL wakes, stretches slowly, then stands with her eyes closed, her arms reaching up and her face tilted into the sun. She touches her cheeks lightly with her fingertips, making light kissing

sounds. She plays with new sounds to describe the feel of the sun:)

TOMATO PLANT GIRL

Firrre—
kissss!

(LITTLE GIRL rushes in, carrying the flowerpot, the watering can, and her book, Tales of Tomatoes.*)*

LITTLE GIRL

Tomato Plant Girl—
(Seeing TOMATO PLANT GIRL in the sun.) Hey! Hey careful!
(LITTLE GIRL stands in front of TOMATO PLANT GIRL, blocking the sun. TOMATO PLANT GIRL tries to move around her. LITTLE GIRL doesn't let her.)
The ultraviolent rays! Sunburn is *wrong.*

TOMATO PLANT GIRL

(reaches for the flowerpot and watering can)
Drink. Dirt!

LITTLE GIRL

Okay!
(LITTLE GIRL gives TOMATO PLANT GIRL dirt and water. TOMATO PLANT GIRL eats and drinks quickly, avidly.)
Tomato Plant Girl: this is important!

TOMATO PLANT GIRL *(satisfied)*

Ahhh.

(TOMATO PLANT GIRL tilts her head back to the sun.)
(To herself.) Firrre—

LITTLE GIRL
Listen! You're going to be my best friend!

TOMATO PLANT GIRL *(to herself)*
kisss ...

LITTLE GIRL
You're going to come home and live with me! We'll go to
school and play games every day—and no one will know
you're a *(lowers her voice)* —foreigner. See?
  *(TOMATO PLANT GIRL looks down at herself, looks back
  at LITTLE GIRL.)*
Come on! I'll show you my house! Let's go!

TOMATO PLANT GIRL *(not moving)*
Root. I.

LITTLE GIRL
You can wash, and dress, and eat normal food—and bor-
row my books! I'll teach you to read!
  (LITTLE GIRL holds out the book.)
I'll teach you to be like a real normal girl so you can be my
best friend and be happy!

TOMATO PLANT GIRL
  (looks at LITTLE GIRL, shakes her head)
Grow.

LITTLE GIRL *(tries not to cry)*

My best friend's coming back, and she's going to be angry!
If you're not my best friend, I'll be all alone!

*(TOMATO PLANT GIRL looks at LITTLE GIRL, picks
up a handful of dirt, shows it to her.)*

TOMATO PLANT GIRL

Grow I.

LITTLE GIRL *(hurt)*

Fine then! You grow!
*(Hurt, LITTLE GIRL turns away from TOMATO PLANT
GIRL. She opens her book, tries to read. TOMATO PLANT
GIRL knows something is wrong.)*

TOMATO PLANT GIRL

Sorry ...

LITTLE GIRL

What?

TOMATO PLANT GIRL

Sor-ry!
(TOMATO PLANT GIRL tugs on the book.)
Mmm.

LITTLE GIRL *(still hurt)*

It's just a book.

TOMATO PLANT GIRL *(points at the cover)*

Red.

(She makes the "BIG" gesture.)
TOMATO!
    (LITTLE GIRL smiles in spite of herself.)
TO-MA-TO!
    *(TOMATO PLANT GIRL sweeps the book out of LITTLE
    GIRL's hands, dances with it.)*
TOMATO!

LITTLE GIRL

HEY! That's my book!
    (LITTLE GIRL takes the book back.)
I'm glad you like it—but you can say "please."

TOMATO PLANT GIRL

Plse.

LITTLE GIRL

It means, "If it pleases you."
    (LITTLE GIRL holds out the book.)
Say you want this book. But the book is mine; it's precious
to me. So I need you to ask and say "please."

    *(TOMATO PLANT GIRL points at the book, naming it
    "Please.")*

TOMATO PLANT GIRL

Please!

LITTLE GIRL

No...
    (LITTLE GIRL decides to demonstrate.)
Here. Hold it. Just for a second.

(Carefully, LITTLE GIRL hands TOMATO PLANT GIRL the book. TOMATO PLANT GIRL holds the book carefully, watching LITTLE GIRL. LITTLE GIRL points at the book.)

Book.

(LITTLE GIRL pretends to admire the book.)

Mmm!

(LITTLE GIRL gestures toward the book, asking permission.)

Please?

(TOMATO PLANT GIRL hands LITTLE GIRL the book.)

Yes! That's right!

(Excited, TOMATO PLANT GIRL does a sped-up, auto-version of the previous actions.)

TOMATO PLANT GIRL

Book—Mmm! *Please?*

(Skeptical, LITTLE GIRL holds the book out to TOMATO PLANT GIRL. TOMATO PLANT GIRL grabs onto it.)

Yezatsright!

LITTLE GIRL *(takes the book back)*

If you say "please" but you don't really mean it, then it's just like you're grabbing the book. But if you say "please" and you really *do* mean it, then I have a choice. I can give you the book.

(TOMATO PLANT GIRL looks at LITTLE GIRL. Motions to the book.)

TOMATO PLANT GIRL

Please?

LITTLE GIRL

Yes!
   (LITTLE GIRL hands TOMATO PLANT GIRL the book.)
Thank you for asking!

   (TOMATO PLANT GIRL gently touches the page, then lifts and turns it. She sees something.)

TOMATO PLANT GIRL

Ahh—firre!

   (TOMATO PLANT GIRL buries her head in the book. LITTLE GIRL reaches toward the book.

LITTLE GIRL

Fire? Let me see!
   (TOMATO PLANT GIRL looks at LITTLE GIRL.)
Please?
   (TOMATO PLANT GIRL shows LITTLE GIRL the picture.)
Oh! That's the sun!
   (LITTLE GIRL points at the sky.)
Remember, I told you—it's dangerous!

TOMATO PLANT GIRL *(points at the sky)*

Firrrekisss!
   (TOMATO PLANT GIRL tilts her face to the sky. Then she remembers the book and carefully hands it back to LITTLE GIRL before stretching into the sun, as before.)
Mmm.

(Intrigued but still concerned, LITTLE GIRL moves between TOMATO PLANT GIRL and the sun.)

LITTLE GIRL

The sun is *ultraviolent.*

TOMATO PLANT GIRL
(calling LITTLE GIRL by her name)

Sorry.

(TOMATO PLANT GIRL moves around LITTLE GIRL, back into the sun. Then she has an idea. She turns back to LITTLE GIRL. She points to the spot next to her.)

Root you.

Please.

(LITTLE GIRL, wary, moves toward TOMATO PLANT GIRL. TOMATO PLANT GIRL shares her "Firekiss" gestures with LITTLE GIRL: she stretches into the sun, then does the sun-kissing gesture and sound.)

Fiire

kiss.

LITTLE GIRL
(watching TOMATO PLANT GIRL)

Firekiss.

(Slowly, LITTLE GIRL tilts her head into the sun.)

Mmm.

(LITTLE GIRL does the sun-kissing gesture and sound.)

TOMATO PLANT GIRL

Mmm!

LITTLE GIRL

Firekiss!

(LITTLE GIRL takes off her hat. They stand there for a moment, side by side. They speak separately, but at the same time:)

LITTLE GIRL, TOMATO PLANT GIRL

Fiirre ... kisss!

(Sound of quick, rhythmic ticking. LITTLE GIRL jumps. BOSSY BEST FRIEND calls from offstage.)

BOSSY BEST FRIEND *(offstage)*

Hello-o! I'm back! Who missed me?

LITTLE GIRL

Oh no!

(LITTLE GIRL looks around, panicked. TOMATO PLANT GIRL thinks it's a game, mirrors her.)

TOMATO PLANT GIRL

Oh no!

LITTLE GIRL

Tomato Plant Girl! Over here!

(LITTLE GIRL crouches down. TOMATO PLANT GIRL crouches down too. LITTLE GIRL hands the book to TOMATO PLANT GIRL, then stands in front of her, attempting to block her from view. BOSSY BEST FRIEND

sails in like a queen. She wears fancy new clothes and carries her bag. She makes a big show of closing her eyes and breathing in the air of the garden.)

BOSSY BEST FRIEND

Ahh. Lovely to be back.

(BOSSY BEST FRIEND opens her eyes. LITTLE GIRL waves with forced enthusiasm, still trying to hide TO-MATO PLANT GIRL.)

LITTLE GIRL

Hello. Hi!

BOSSY BEST FRIEND

I'm early. I know. I was worried, poor dear. You've been here all alone—
    (BOSSY BEST FRIEND sees her plant is gone.)
Where's my plant? Did you let it die?

LITTLE GIRL

You said not to touch it!

BOSSY BEST FRIEND

You should have known better!

(TOMATO PLANT GIRL, still hidden, points at a picture in the book.)

TOMATO PLANT GIRL

RED!

(BOSSY BEST FRIEND hears the sound; LITTLE GIRL tries to distract her and block TOMATO PLANT GIRL.)

LITTLE GIRL *(loudly)*
Yes! You're right! I'm very sorry!

(BOSSY BEST FRIEND moves LITTLE GIRL aside. Shocked, she stares at TOMATO PLANT GIRL)

BOSSY BEST FRIEND
Who's that thing.

LITTLE GIRL
She's new.

BOSSY BEST FRIEND
She's *repulsive*.

LITTLE GIRL
She's nice.

BOSSY BEST FRIEND
She's got that dumb book.

(TOMATO PLANT GIRL stares, fascinated, at BOSSY BEST FRIEND. LITTLE GIRL tries to take the book from TOMATO PLANT GIRL, who holds on.)

LITTLE GIRL
Tomato Plant Girl—

BOSSY BEST FRIEND

"Tomato Plant Girl"?

LITTLE GIRL

—please give me the book!

(TOMATO PLANT GIRL lets LITTLE GIRL have the book. Still watching TOMATO PLANT GIRL, BOSSY BEST FRIEND sweeps the book away from LITTLE GIRL.)

BOSSY BEST FRIEND

Thank you.

(BOSSY BEST FRIEND puts the book in her bag. LITTLE GIRL watches, upset, but says nothing. BOSSY BEST FRIEND clears her throat, suddenly very polite.)

Excuse me, you grimy strange girl. You're in my garden. I'd like to know who you are.

(BOSSY BEST FRIEND summons TOMATO PLANT GIRL with a wave. TOMATO PLANT GIRL moves toward her, intrigued, imitating the wave.)

LITTLE GIRL

There's nothing wrong with her. She's new.

(BOSSY BEST FRIEND walks slowly around TOMATO PLANT GIRL, inspecting her at a slight distance.)

BOSSY BEST FRIEND

Mmm-hmm—mmm-hmm—mmm-hmm.

(TOMATO PLANT GIRL notices the bow on BOSSY BEST FRIEND's dress. She becomes entranced. She tugs at and unties it, makes a sound of delight. BOSSY BEST FRIEND gasps, whirls around. TOMATO PLANT GIRL looks at her, innocent. LITTLE GIRL starts to laugh. BOSSY BEST FRIEND turns back to LITTLE GIRL, furious.)

BOSSY BEST FRIEND

Booknose—
(LITTLE GIRL stands at attention.)
Come here.

(BOSSY BEST FRIEND motions for LITTLE GIRL to stand behind her and tie the bow. She does, but sneaks a look at TOMATO PLANT GIRL. TOMATO PLANT GIRL stands up close, facing BOSSY BEST FRIEND, and stares at her.)

BOSSY BEST FRIEND

You're *dirty*.

TOMATO PLANT GIRL *(gleeful)*

DIRRT!

(BOSSY BEST FRIEND stamps her foot, turns to LITTLE GIRL, points at her watch.)

BOSSY BEST FRIEND

It's five-o-five. Barbie time. Now.
(BOSSY BEST FRIEND snaps her fingers once, then points for LITTLE GIRL to set up the game. She does. BOSSY BEST FRIEND holds out LITTLE GIRL's Barbie.

TOMATO PLANT GIRL stands between them and watches, fascinated.)

BOSSY BEST FRIEND

You're this one.

LITTLE GIRL

I know.

BOSSY BEST FRIEND

One—two—
(To TOMATO PLANT GIRL.) Move away, please!

TOMATO PLANT GIRL *(recognizing the word)*

Please!

LITTLE GIRL *(to BOSSY BEST FRIEND)*

She can watch.

BOSSY BEST FRIEND *(glaring)*

One. Two. Three.

(LITTLE GIRL is quiet. During the next lines, TOMATO PLANT GIRL hovers over BOSSY BEST FRIEND's shoulder, moving her head with the rhythm of the words. LITTLE GIRL plays with one eye on TOMATO PLANT GIRL.)

BOSSY BEST FRIEND

Dena!

LITTLE GIRL

Lena!
(Three loud, fakey kisses.)
How are you?

BOSSY BEST FRIEND

Terrific.

LITTLE GIRL

And your job?

BOSSY BEST FRIEND

Perfecto.

LITTLE GIRL

And your boyfriends?

BOSSY BEST FRIEND

Too fine.

LITTLE GIRL

You look—

TOMATO PLANT GIRL

HA!

(TOMATO PLANT GIRL plucks the Barbie from BOSSY BEST FRIEND's hand. She shakes the Barbie around until its hair is big and messy. Then she puts the Barbie's feet in her mouth. BOSSY BEST FRIEND grabs the Barbie and points it at TOMATO PLANT GIRL.)

BOSSY BEST FRIEND

You stop that and say sorry!

TOMATO PLANT GIRL *(to LITTLE GIRL)*

Sorry?

LITTLE GIRL

Never mind. It's okay.
   *(LITTLE GIRL starts to show TOMATO PLANT GIRL
   how to hold Barbie.)*
Here. Watch.

*(BOSSY BEST FRIEND takes LITTLE GIRL's Barbie
from her hand and moves her aside.)*

BOSSY BEST FRIEND

Excuse me. Thank you.
   *(BOSSY BEST FRIEND stands next to TOMATO PLANT
   GIRL and smiles, holding up LITTLE GIRL's Barbie.)*
This is how we play with Barbie. Like this. Feet. Head.
(Smoothing the hair.) Hair. In place. Then: arrange Barbie.

*(BOSSY BEST FRIEND puts the Barbie's arms in a
proper position. She hands it to TOMATO PLANT GIRL.
LITTLE GIRL watches. TOMATO PLANT GIRL holds
the Barbie right side up, pats her hair, then starts to
move her into an odd position.)*

LITTLE GIRL *(correcting her)*

No, like this—

(BOSSY BEST FRIEND glares at LITTLE GIRL.)

BOSSY BEST FRIEND *(to TOMATO PLANT GIRL)*
You're such a fast learner. That's lovely.
   *(BOSSY BEST FRIEND takes the Barbie and hands it
   back to TOMATO PLANT GIRL. LITTLE GIRL watches,
   frustrated.)*
Now. One-two-three. *(As her own Barbie.)* Dena! *(Pointing
at TOMATO PLANT GIRL's Barbie.)* Lena!

TOMATO PLANT GIRL

LEEENA!

BOSSY BEST FRIEND *(as herself)*
Beautiful. Now—

TOMATO PLANT GIRL

LEENA LEENA—

LITTLE GIRL *(starting to join her)*

LEENA—

BOSSY BEST FRIEND *(to LITTLE GIRL)*
Stop! *(To TOMATO PLANT GIRL.)* Lena. That's right.
   *(BOSSY BEST FRIEND takes the Barbie and keeps it
   away from TOMATO PLANT GIRL.)*
Now watch. One-two-three.
   (BOSSY BEST FRIEND demonstrates with both Barbies.)
Dena!
Lena!
   (Kiss-kiss-kiss.)
How are you?
Just *terrific.*
And your job?

Perfecto.
And your boyfriends?
Too—

(TOMATO PLANT GIRL picks up a stick from the ground and holds it up proudly between the Barbies, as if it is a doll. This is her way of playing.)

TOMATO PLANT GIRL

Stick!

BOSSY BEST FRIEND

Stop it! *(Handing LITTLE GIRL her Barbie.)* Tell her to stop.

TOMATO PLANT GIRL
(as Stick, to the other Barbies)

Stick Bar-bieee! Stick I!
(TOMATO PLANT GIRL kisses LITTLE GIRL's Barbie on the cheek.)

LITTLE GIRL *(as her Barbie)*

Oh! Hello Stick!

(TOMATO PLANT GIRL repeats "Stick" over and over, moving around BOSSY BEST FRIEND and LITTLE GIRL.)

BOSSY BEST FRIEND *(to LITTLE GIRL)*

Stop playing like that! *(As her Barbie.)* Now listen, Stick—

TOMATO PLANT GIRL *(to LITTLE GIRL)*

Terrrriffic! Stick I!

LITTLE GIRL *(as her Barbie)*
Perfecto! Too fine!

BOSSY BEST FRIEND *(to LITTLE GIRL)*
You're doing it wrong!
(BOSSY BEST FRIEND takes LITTLE GIRL's Barbie and blocks TOMATO PLANT GIRL's way.)
Stop playing with her! I'm your friend!

LITTLE GIRL
She's my friend too!

BOSSY BEST FRIEND
I'm your friend.

LITTLE GIRL *(matter-of-fact)*
And she's my—

BOSSY BEST FRIEND
Dumb Booknose. Dumb *foreigner* girl!

(LITTLE GIRL freezes.)

TOMATO PLANT GIRL *(in LITTLE GIRL's face)*
Stick!!

LITTLE GIRL *(to TOMATO PLANT GIRL)*
STOP. Stop that now.
(LITTLE GIRL grabs Stick Barbie out of TOMATO PLANT GIRL's hand. TOMATO PLANT GIRL makes an indignant noise.)

This is *not* how we play. It's loud and dangerous. *Now sit over there and calm down. Right now.*
  (Cornered, TOMATO PLANT GIRL bites LITTLE GIRL's pointing finger in self-defense, then runs off.)
(Shocked.) Ow!
Tomato Plant Girl—wait!

(LITTLE GIRL starts to go after TOMATO PLANT GIRL. BOSSY BEST FRIEND blocks her way.)

BOSSY BEST FRIEND

Don't.

LITTLE GIRL

But I—

BOSSY BEST FRIEND

You did the right thing.
  (Holding up LITTLE GIRL's Barbie.)
You're this one.
  (LITTLE GIRL doesn't take it.)
You're *this* one.

(LITTLE GIRL makes a decision. She takes her Barbie, looks at BOSSY BEST FRIEND.)

LITTLE GIRL

I know.

BOSSY BEST FRIEND

One—two—three!

(BOSSY BEST FRIEND speaks as her Barbie.)
Dena!

(LITTLE GIRL plays, ignoring BOSSY BEST FRIEND's game.)

LITTLE GIRL

Root!

BOSSY BEST FRIEND

Don't I look *stunning?*

LITTLE GIRL

Dirrrt.

BOSSY BEST FRIEND

My job is divine!

LITTLE GIRL

Fiire—

BOSSY BEST FRIEND *(furious)*

That's a horrible dress!

LITTLE GIRL

—*kissssun!*

(BOSSY BEST FRIEND grabs LITTLE GIRL's Barbie.)

BOSSY BEST FRIEND

Your Barbie wants what my Barbie wants but my Barbie can have it and your Barbie—

LITTLE GIRL

No!

BOSSY BEST FRIEND

That's the game.

LITTLE GIRL

Your game.

BOSSY BEST FRIEND

Our game!

LITTLE GIRL

Your game. I don't like it.
   *(BOSSY BEST FRIEND starts to speak. LITTLE GIRL
   steps forward.)*
And I didn't like you taking my book or making me give
you your plant!

BOSSY BEST FRIEND

Making you?

LITTLE GIRL

Yes!

BOSSY BEST FRIEND

I said "please"!

LITTLE GIRL

You didn't mean it!

BOSSY BEST FRIEND
Fine. Never mind. We'll play Mother May I.

(BOSSY BEST FRIEND claps twice. LITTLE GIRL picks up the stick.)

LITTLE GIRL
Stick!
(LITTLE GIRL spins and plays with the stick.)

BOSSY BEST FRIEND
Put it down.

LITTLE GIRL *(still playing)*
No.

BOSSY BEST FRIEND *(grabs hold of the stick)*
Little Girl: I'm your *friend!*

LITTLE GIRL *(matter-of-fact)*
No.
(LITTLE GIRL lets go of the stick.)
You're not.

BOSSY BEST FRIEND
Booknose: be careful. Your other friend's gone.

LITTLE GIRL *(uncertain)*
Then—I'll play alone.

BOSSY BEST FRIEND *(scornful)*
You'll play *alone?*

LITTLE GIRL *(more confident)*

I'll play alone.

(BOSSY BEST FRIEND drops the stick on the ground. She picks up her Barbies and bag and turns to go.)

LITTLE GIRL

Wait—

BOSSY BEST FRIEND *(turns back, expectant)*

Yes?

LITTLE GIRL

My book. *(Respectfully.)* Please.

(Crushed, BOSSY BEST FRIEND glares at LITTLE GIRL. BOSSY BEST FRIEND takes the book from her bag and holds it high in the air.)

BOSSY BEST FRIEND

Dumb boring foreigner book!

(BOSSY BEST FRIEND drops the book. LITTLE GIRL catches it.)

Have fun alone!

(BOSSY BEST FRIEND turns on her heel and exits. LITTLE GIRL hugs the book.)

LITTLE GIRL *(to herself)*

I'll play alone.

(Pause. LITTLE GIRL looks around her, uncertain.)

Alone.

(Calling.) Tomato Plant Girl?
(LITTLE GIRL takes a deep breath and closes her eyes, gathering courage.)
I'll play alone.
(LITTLE GIRL breathes deep, eyes closed, hugging the book.)

(TOMATO PLANT GIRL enters. She is fully grown: a red, round tomato. But she is still hurt and wary of LIT-TLE GIRL. She approaches LITTLE GIRL and gently taps her shoulder. LITTLE GIRL jumps, looks at TO-MATO PLANT GIRL.)

LITTLE GIRL

Tomato Plant Girl! Wow! Look at you!

TOMATO PLANT GIRL

Grow I.

(Pause. They look at each other, then away. They start to speak at the same time.)

LITTLE GIRL	TOMATO PLANT GIRL
(an apology)	*(LITTLE GIRL's name)*
I'm sorry.	Sorry—

(They laugh for a moment.)

LITTLE GIRL

I should have, but I didn't. I shouldn't have, but I did.

(TOMATO PLANT GIRL points at LITTLE GIRL, imitating her reprimand.)

TOMATO PLANT GIRL
Sitoverthere! SitoverthereNOW!

LITTLE GIRL
I didn't know what to do.

(TOMATO PLANT GIRL imitates BOSSY BEST FRIEND yelling "Foreigner!" at LITTLE GIRL.)

TOMATO PLANT GIRL
"Forrner!"
(TOMATO PLANT GIRL imitates LITTLE GIRL gasping in shock.)

LITTLE GIRL
I *like* being a foreigner! That's why I like you. That's why I'm your friend.

TOMATO PLANT GIRL *(unsure of the meaning)*
Frrrend.

LITTLE GIRL
Someone who...knows who you are. And likes you. All of you.
(Pause.)
Are you still my friend?

(TOMATO PLANT GIRL takes LITTLE GIRL's hand and kisses the finger she bit earlier.)

TOMATO PLANT GIRL

Frrrend.

(LITTLE GIRL starts to cry and laugh at the same time. TOMATO PLANT GIRL starts to cry/laugh too. TO-MATO PLANT GIRL lifts her index finger and reaches out toward LITTLE GIRL's face. LITTLE GIRL slowly does the same. At the same moment, each wipes a tear from the other's cheek. LITTLE GIRL tastes TOMATO PLANT GIRL's tear.)

LITTLE GIRL

Friend.

(TOMATO PLANT GIRL tastes LITTLE GIRL's tear.)

TOMATO PLANT GIRL

Friend.

(They stand facing each other a moment.)

LITTLE GIRL

Tomato Plant Girl—

TOMATO PLANT GIRL

Grow I.

LITTLE GIRL

I know.

TOMATO PLANT GIRL

Errth.

LITTLE GIRL *(remembering)*
Plants go back to the earth ... to feed other plants.
(To TOMATO PLANT GIRL.) You have to go back, don't
you?

TOMATO PLANT GIRL *(affirming)*
Errth.

LITTLE GIRL
(holds out her book to TOMATO PLANT GIRL)
Here. I want you to have it.

TOMATO PLANT GIRL *(takes the book)*
Red!

LITTLE GIRL
It's a gift.

TOMATO PLANT GIRL
Gifft.
(Thanking her.) Tomato.
*(TOMATO PLANT GIRL hugs the book, accepting it. She
motions to LITTLE GIRL.)*
Root you. Please.
*(TOMATO PLANT GIRL scoops up handfuls of dirt from
LITTLE GIRL's side of the garden. She begins to hum as
she sprinkles the dirt onto LITTLE GIRL.)*
Grow you.
Gift.

*(LITTLE GIRL smiles, rubs the dirt on her hands and
face.)*

LITTLE GIRL

Gift.

(The Earthsoil Hum returns.)

The Earth hum!

(LITTLE GIRL acknowledges the Earthsoil Hum with TO-MATO PLANT GIRL's gesture. TOMATO PLANT GIRL joins her in the gesture and the hum. They continue to hum, transforming the gesture, once, then twice. The second time, they join hands. They spin in a circle, facing each other.)

LITTLE GIRL

Tomatosweetleafplantreadyonetwo!

(LITTLE GIRL drops a hand. They hold on by one.)

Velvet green and flower-sun gold!

In root, in heart, in sun—

alone!

(LITTLE GIRL lets TOMATO PLANT GIRL go. TO-MATO PLANT GIRL spins off and folds back into the earth at the same spot where she emerged. LITTLE GIRL stops spinning.)

Alone. I'll play alone.

(LITTLE GIRL looks at the place where TOMATO PLANT GIRL disappeared. She picks up two handfuls of earth and sprinkles it over the spot. Then she stretches up and spins, breathing out. She reaches up and lets the earth fall through her fingers.)

Gift I.

Grow I.

Grow I.

(In the place where TOMATO PLANT GIRL folded into the earth, a new tomato plant springs up, healthy and green, with a single red tomato.)

END OF PLAY

DIRECTOR'S NOTES

DIRECTOR'S NOTES